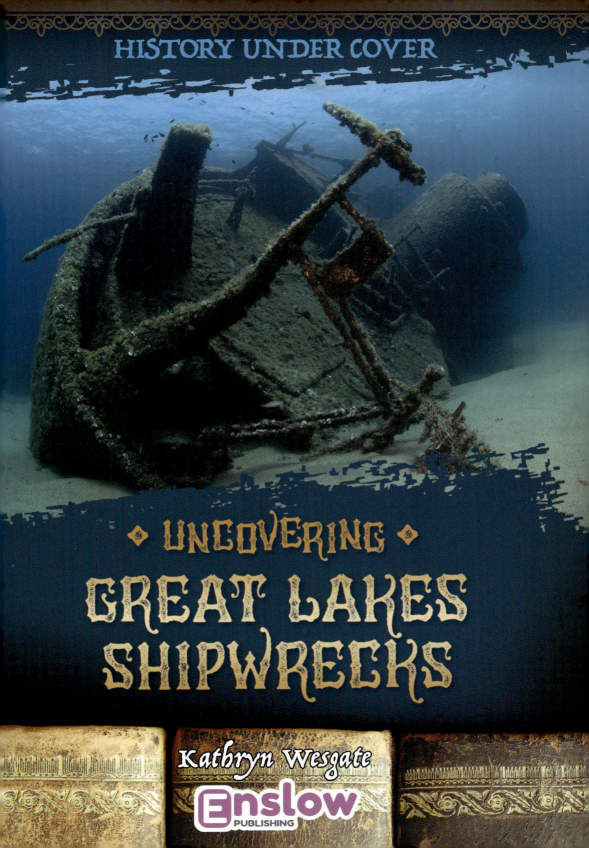

Please visit our website, www.enslow.com. For a free color catalog of all our high-quality books, call toll free 1-800-398-2504 or fax 1-877-980-4454.

Library of Congress Cataloging-in-Publication Data
Names: Wesgate, Kathryn, author.
Title: Uncovering Great Lakes shipwrecks / Kathryn Wesgate.
Description: New York : Enslow Publishing, 2023. | Series: History under cover | Includes index.
Identifiers: LCCN 2021050643 | ISBN 9781978528833 (set) | ISBN 9781978528840 (library binding) | ISBN 9781978528826 (paperback) | ISBN 9781978528857 (ebook)
Subjects: LCSH: Shipwrecks–Great Lakes (North America)–History–Juvenile literature. | Great Lakes Region (North America)–History, Naval–Juvenile literature.
Classification: LCC G525 .W4226 2023 | DDC 917.704–dc23/eng/20211217
LC record available at https://lccn.loc.gov/2021050643

Published in 2023 by
Enslow Publishing
29 East 21st Street
New York, NY 10010

Copyright © 2023 Enslow Publishing

Portions of this work were originally authored by Melissa Raé Shofner and published as *Great Lakes Shipwrecks*. All new material this edition authored by Kathryn Wesgate.

Designer: Leslie Taylor
Editor: Kate Mikoley

Photo credits: Cover, Pinosub/Shutterstock.com, series art (scrolls) Magenta10/Shutterstock.com, series art (back cover leather texture) levan828/Shutterstock.com; series art (front cover books) RMMPPhotography/Shutterstock.com; series art (title font) MagicPics/Shutterstock.com; series art (ripped inside pgs) kaczor58/Shutterstock.com; p. 4 commons.wikimedia.org/wiki/File:John_V._Moran_6.jpg; p. 5 (bottom) Vismar UK/Shutterstock.com; p. 5 (map) Rainer Lesniewski/Shutterstock.com; p. 6 Kenneth Keifer/Shutterstock.com; p. 7 (top) Tribune Conent Agency LLC / Alamy.com; p. 7 (bottom) GL Archive/Alamy.com; p. 8 Tim Kornoelje/Shutterstock.com; p. 9 commons.wikimedia.org/wiki/File:Nov291905LifeSavingCrew.jpg; p. 9 (top) commons.wikimedia.org/wiki/File:Mataafa.jpg; p. 10 Richard Whitcombe/Shutterstock.com; p. 11 Shane Gross/Shutterstock.com; p. 12 Drew McArthur/Shutterstock.com; p. 13 Jellyman Photography/Shutterstock.com; p. 13 (inset) commons.wikimedia.org/wiki/File:Poster_-_20,000_Leagues_under_the_Sea_(1916).jpg; p. 14 commons.wikimedia.org/wiki/File:Shipwreck_Francisco_Morazan_04.jpg; p. 14 (inset) commons.wikimedia.org/wiki/File:SS_Milwaukee.jpg; p. 15 MP cz/Shutterstock.com; p. 16 AB Forces News Collection/Alamy.com; p. 17 commons.wikimedia.org/wiki/File:Steamer_Penobscot.jpg; p. 18 commons.wikimedia.org/wiki/File:MONOHANSETT_(15361605032).jpg; p. 19 John McCormick/Shutterstock.com; p. 20 Carol M. Highsmith/LOC; p. 21 commons.wikimedia.org/wiki/File:SS_Hydrus.jpg; p. 22 Dan Leeth/Alamy.com; p. 23 Bruce Montagne/Dembinsky Photo Associates/Alamy.com; p. 23 (stamp) catwalker/Shutterstock.com; p. 23 (ship bell) Dianne Leeth/Alamy.com; p. 24 Kibrok Photography/Shutterstock.com; p. 25 Drew McArthur/Shutterstock.com; p. 26 Jeff Caughey/Shutterstock.com; p. 27 DJ Mattaar/Shutterstock.com; p. 27 (inset) Hunter Watson Photography/Shutterstock.com; p. 28 Terry Reimink/Shutterstock.com; p. 29 Carlos Osorio/APimages.com.

All rights reserved. No part of this book may be reproduced in any form without permission in writing from the publisher, except by a reviewer.

Printed in the United States of America

Some of the images in this book illustrate individuals who are models. The depictions do not imply actual situations or events.

CPSIA compliance information: Batch #CSENS23: For further information, contact Enslow Publishing, New York, New York, at 1-800-398-2504.

Find us on

Underwater History 4
About the Lakes 6
Rough Waters 8
Underwater Investigating 10
Strange Cargo 14
Danger on Board 16
A Steamer Sinks 18
The Great Storm of 1913 20
The *Edmund Fitzgerald* 22
Shallow Shipwrecks 24
Shipwreck Pests 26
Shipwrecks at Risk 28
Glossary 30
For More Information 31
Index 32

Words in the glossary appear in bold or highlighted type the first time they are used in the text.

Underwater History

You've probably heard of shipwrecks happening at sea, but the ocean isn't the only place where shipwrecks occur. In fact, unpredictable, or uncertain, weather makes the Great Lakes some of the most dangerous waters in the world.

One example of a shipwreck on the Great Lakes is the *John V. Moran*, a steamship that carried flour and other goods. One night in February 1899, the ship's hull was damaged by ice in Lake Michigan. A nearby boat rescued the crew. When it returned the next day to tow the *Moran* to shore, it was clear the ship couldn't be saved. Left to sink, the *Moran* wouldn't be seen again for 116 years.

the *John V. Moran*

This is just one of several thousand stories of shipwrecks in the Great Lakes since the 1600s. Much history hides within these lakes!

4

The Great Lakes

Experts estimate that there have been more than 6,000 shipwrecks and 30,000 related deaths in the Great Lakes.

~ Preserved In Place ~

On June 4, 2015, a team from the Michigan Shipwreck Research Association (MSRA) picked up a shipwreck on its sonar. They used a remotely operated vehicle, or ROV, to record video of the wreck. It turned out to be the *John V. Moran*. Surprisingly, after sitting at the bottom of Lake Michigan for more than 100 years, the ship was in near-perfect condition. It appeared to be missing only one piece! Craig Rich, a historian and diver who saw the ROV video, said the ship looked like it was just "waiting to sail away."

About the Lakes

There are five Great Lakes: Superior, Michigan, Huron, Erie, and Ontario. They are all found in the northeastern United States. Lake Huron, Lake Superior, Lake Erie, and Lake Ontario share borders with Canada, but Lake Michigan is located completely in the United States.

Around 14,000 years ago, a glacier covered the area and formed the lakes. The glacier carved out the lakes as it melted and moved across the region. Today, the Great Lakes cover about 95,000 square miles (246,050 sq km) and hold more than 5,400 cubic miles (22,500 cu km) of water.

Many rivers and smaller waterways connect the five lakes. Together, the Great Lakes form the largest system of fresh water on the planet. About 20 percent of Earth's fresh surface water is found here.

Lake Superior

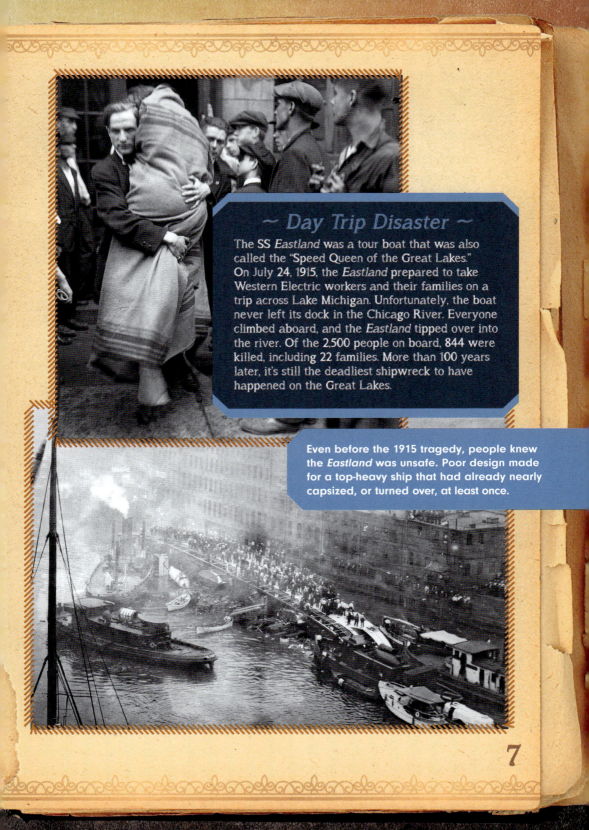

~ Day Trip Disaster ~

The SS *Eastland* was a tour boat that was also called the "Speed Queen of the Great Lakes." On July 24, 1915, the *Eastland* prepared to take Western Electric workers and their families on a trip across Lake Michigan. Unfortunately, the boat never left its dock in the Chicago River. Everyone climbed aboard, and the *Eastland* tipped over into the river. Of the 2,500 people on board, 844 were killed, including 22 families. More than 100 years later, it's still the deadliest shipwreck to have happened on the Great Lakes.

Even before the 1915 tragedy, people knew the *Eastland* was unsafe. Poor design made for a top-heavy ship that had already nearly capsized, or turned over, at least once.

Rough Waters

Strong winds, big waves, and cold air have covered this lighthouse on Lake Michigan with a thick layer of ice. During colder months, this can happen to ships on the Great Lakes too.

The Great Lakes are home to more than 30,000 islands. Many of these are very small. The Great Lakes and their connecting rivers also feature rocky reefs. To make way for large ships, people sometimes clear away reefs. In some places, however, new, man-made reefs are being constructed to help fish populations that have been dying out without reefs.

Navigating around islands and reefs of the Great Lakes can be difficult for ships, especially during severe weather. Storm systems over the lakes can create strong winds, which in turn create large waves. Warm lake waters and cold air can also cause heavy, unpredictable snowstorms. When temperatures become cold enough, ice can also be a major problem for ships. Large pieces of ice in the water can damage ships if hit.

~ Witches of November ~

Historically, November is a bad month for shipwrecks on the Great Lakes. Warm waters and cold air from Canada often combine around this time. Strong storms, called "November witches," sometimes develop. These storms can bring hail, icy rain, snow, and even hurricane-force winds to the lakes. The 1905 "*Mataafa* Storm" is a famous November witch named for a tragic shipwreck on Lake Superior. People watched from the shoreline as the SS *Mataafa* was torn apart, just out of reach of rescuers. Nine men died in the wreck.

SS *Mataafa*

This image shows a crew rowing toward the *Mataafa* wreck in an effort to rescue survivors.

9

Underwater Investigating

Underwater archaeologists dive into the Great Lakes to study shipwrecks. They learn how people and goods were once transported over the Great Lakes by studying ships that sank there. They can also figure out how the ships were built and what caused them to sink.

Most tools used in underwater archaeology are similar to those used on dry land. Scientists **document** wrecks using waterproof paper called Mylar and regular pencils. One special underwater tool is a vacuum-like hose called a dredge. This tool sucks up water and sediment. A floating screen sifts the sediment to catch small pieces of bone or **artifacts**.

Not everyone who studies shipwrecks is a scientist, however. Many amateur divers explore shipwrecks too! Some shipwrecks have become popular attractions for recreational divers looking to explore the Great Lakes.

When a shipwreck remains in one place for years, it often becomes a **habitat** for many plants and animals.

~ Lessons on the Environment ~

Shipwrecks don't only reveal information about history. They can also tell us more about the environment. By studying wrecks in the Great Lakes, we can learn about the currents of a particular lake. For example, scientists have found that the waters of Lake Michigan move in an unusual and slow circular pattern. Shipwrecks also show us how human error and technology can change and sometimes damage the environment. Sunken ships become part of the underwater environment, and biologists study the organisms that live around wrecks.

11

    Large vessels began sailing the Great Lakes in the 17th century, so shipwrecks here are a bit like sunken **time capsules**. Older wrecks may contain artifacts hundreds of years old. Unlike other historical sites such as temples or graves, there's no time for arrangement during a shipwreck. Shipwrecks offer a historical snapshot of the moment the wreck occurred.

    Because artifacts are clues that help unlock the mysteries of the past, amateur divers must not move or take them from shipwrecks. When studying a wreck, scientists document one section at a time in great detail. They make drawings and take notes, photographs, and video to record a ship's story. Often many questions remain even after a ship's discovery. Even the most experienced scientists can't always tell why a ship sank.

It can be dangerous for divers to swim inside a shipwreck. Many explorers stay in the waters outside the sunken vessels.

~ James Lockwood ~

James Lockwood was a Great Lakes shipwreck explorer. He was also a diving pioneer. He made his own diving equipment, created an underwater camera case for the 1930s Tarzan movies, and built underwater props for the film *20,000 Leagues Under the Sea*. While in the navy in the 1940s, Lockwood rescued pilots whose planes crashed into Lake Michigan. Lockwood also edited a diving magazine and wrote and lectured about his many inventions and discoveries. The Lockwood School of Diving and Underwater Technology at the College of the Florida Keys is named in his honor.

13

Strange Cargo

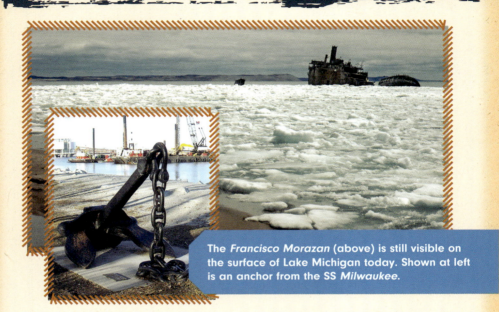

The *Francisco Morazan* (above) is still visible on the surface of Lake Michigan today. Shown at left is an anchor from the SS *Milwaukee*.

Certain shipwrecks have resulted in some odd cargo making its way into the Great Lakes, especially in Lake Michigan. The *Francisco Morazan* ran aground during a blizzard in February 1960. The ship was carrying 2 tons (1.8 mt) of bottle caps, 95 tons (86 mt) of canned chicken, and more than 2 tons of hair, among other odd things. Locals took much of the cargo, and a fire in 1968 destroyed what was left. Today, seabirds live in the wreckage, which remains mostly above water.

In 1929, the SS *Milwaukee* was loaded with 27 train cars that held everything from bathtubs to cheese. The ship set sail—even though the weather was bad—and soon sank. Divers later found that the train cars had broken free and damaged the ship. The train cars remain inside the wreckage, 115 feet (35 m) underwater.

Dry suits, such as the one this diver is wearing, allow divers to stay warm during cold dives.

~ Staying Warm ~

Salty ocean water can cause shipwrecks to deteriorate, or fall apart, but the fresh water of the Great Lakes is cold and keeps most wrecks in excellent condition. While the cold waters are great for preserving the wrecks, they can make it hard for divers to stay warm. To solve this problem, Great Lakes divers usually wear dry suits instead of wet suits. As their names suggest, wet suits let the skin become wet, while dry suits keep it dry. Divers can wear warm clothes beneath dry suits and they will stay completely dry.

Danger on Board

Shipwrecks don't only put the people on board in danger. Some put the whole environment around them at risk. In October 1937, the *Argo* was making her way across Lake Erie when heavy winds kicked up. She wasn't built for the unpredictable weather of the Great Lakes and shouldn't have been allowed to sail the lakes at all. Unable to handle the storm, the *Argo* went missing beneath the waves and was lost for nearly 80 years.

These tanks were made to safely remove the benzol from the *Argo* shipwreck from Lake Erie.

When the *Argo* was found, divers noticed a possibly toxic substance seeping from the wreck. About 100,000 gallons (378,540 L) of benzol solvent, which is similar to paint thinner, was on board. After 2 months of containment and cleanup efforts, crews were able to clean up the area.

~ Fire on Board! ~

On the night of October 29, 1951, the freight barge *Morania* was accidentally towed directly into the path of the *Penobscot*, a steamer. The two ships rammed into each other near the Buffalo River, which empties into the eastern end of Lake Erie. When the *Penobscot* pulled away, the 800,000 gallons (3,028,300 L) of gasoline carried by the *Morania* caught fire. There was an explosion, and 11 crewmen were killed. Many people watched the disaster unfold as the fire raged on for several days after the crash.

On the night of the crash, the crew of the *Penobscot*, shown above, did not see the *Morania* in time to avoid the accident because the *Morania* was not very well lit.

A Steamer Sinks

The **Industrial Revolution** in the United States was fueled in part by ore-carrying ships in the Great Lakes. The wooden steamer *Monohansett* transported iron ore across Lake Superior in the late 1800s. At 167 feet (51 m) long, it was much smaller than the 1,000-foot (305 m) freighters that sail today. However, it was one of the first ships with the basic design elements of modern freighters, including long, open decks and hatches that allowed cargo to be easily poured into the holds below.

The *Monohansett* wreck is located in a shallow part of Lake Huron, making it a popular spot for divers.

In November 1907, the *Monohansett* made it to safety near an island on Lake Huron during a bad storm. In an unlucky twist, a lantern accident sent the ship up in flames. The crew of 12 was saved, but the ship wasn't so lucky. The *Monohansett* sank.

~ Finding a Forest ~

In 1926, the *Herman H. Hettler* smashed into a rock reef in Lake Superior while seeking shelter from a storm. After a second storm, the ship was left to sink. Years later, divers found a tree among the wreckage. Scientific testing determined that the tree was about 7,900 years old! Scientists think a forest may have grown here thousands of years ago when Lake Superior's water levels were lower. Other trees have been discovered in the depths of the lake too, mostly by divers looking for shipwrecks.

Lake Superior

The Great Storm of 1913

In November 1913, two strong storms combined forces and battered the Great Lakes for five long days. This November witch, the worst in the recorded history of the lakes, is known by several names, including the "White Hurricane" and the "Great Storm of 1913." Lake Huron was hit hardest, but there were also major wrecks on Lake Erie, Lake Michigan, and Lake Superior.

The "White Hurricane" of November 1913 killed about 250 people, making it the worst natural disaster to hit the Great Lakes. This monument in Port Huron, Michigan, is a place for people to remember those lost.

A break in the storm on November 9 led many ship captains to believe it was safe to venture back out. By evening, however, the storm was back in full force. Hurricane-force winds and 35-foot (10.7 m) waves made for terribly dangerous conditions. Only a few ships caught in open water were able to survive the storm. Twelve ships went down without survivors.

~ Meet Dave Trotter ~

Dave Trotter is fascinated by the hidden history of the Great Lakes. He's been exploring and documenting shipwrecks for nearly 50 years. In 2015, after searching for 30 years, he located a ship that sank in Lake Huron during the Great Storm of 1913. The *Hydrus* was a steamship that lost all of its 22 crew members in the storm. Trotter also founded the Undersea Research Associates, a group that uses special sonar to create underwater history videos. His work has paved the way for further exploration of the Great Lakes.

The *Hydrus* (pictured above) was one of the ships lost during the Great Storm of 1913. The wreck was finally discovered by Dave Trotter in 2015.

The Edmund Fitzgerald

One of the best-known shipwrecks of all time is also the most recent major shipwreck disaster to occur on the Great Lakes: the *Edmund Fitzgerald*.

The *Fitzgerald* and the *Arthur M. Anderson* were traveling across Lake Superior together on November 10, 1975. A strong storm had been forecast in the area the day before, and the two ships were trying to reach safety. Huge waves and strong winds battered both vessels. The *Anderson* lost sight of the *Fitzgerald*, which was several miles ahead. All 29 men aboard died when the *Fitzgerald* sank. Their bodies were never recovered. It took more than a year for the wreckage to be found, and the exact cause of the sinking hasn't been determined. Many think huge storm waves tore the ship apart.

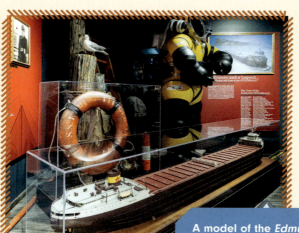

A model of the *Edmund Fitzgerald* is on display at the Great Lakes Shipwreck Museum in Michigan.

This monument for the *Edmund Fitzgerald* is located outside the Great Lakes Shipwreck Museum in Michigan. The ship's bell is also on display at the museum.

~ Honoring the Dead ~

The mystery of what caused the *Fitzgerald* to sink has captured the imaginations of many. The year after the wreck, folk musician Gordon Lightfoot released "The Wreck of the *Edmund Fitzgerald*," which became a hit song.

The wreck also became a popular diving spot. This upset families of the lost crewmen. They didn't want divers bothering their loved ones' final resting place. To honor those lost in the tragedy, the Great Lakes Shipwreck Historical Society gave special permission for the ship's bell to be brought ashore as a memorial.

Shallow Shipwrecks

Lake Superior is the deepest of the Great Lakes. Its deepest point is more than 1,300 feet (396 m). The shallowest is Lake Erie. Its deepest point is about 210 feet (64 m). Some shipwrecks happen in deep, open waters, but many occur just offshore. Some of these wrecks are submerged in shallow water, while others are left partly exposed above the surface. Shallow dive sites are popular because they're easy for amateur divers to explore.

In the spring of 2015, Lake Michigan was very clear. Ice over the lake had melted, but algae had not yet bloomed. U.S. Coast Guard pilots in the area realized they could see more shipwrecks than usual as they flew over the lake. They couldn't all be identified, but one newly discovered wreck dated back to 1848.

This photograph shows a sunken ship close to the surface of Lake Huron.

Properly conserving shipwreck artifacts takes a lot of time and can be quite expensive, but it helps reveal fascinating facts about history.

~ Protecting History ~

Wooden artifacts that are waterlogged, or soaked with water, need special care. This is because wet wood can easily decay, or rot. When a wooden artifact is removed from water, it needs to be kept wet, just as it was found. In the lab, scientists use conservation methods, sometimes involving chemicals, when drying and restoring the artifacts to protect them from further decay. Conservation is time-consuming and can cost a lot of money. However, long-term preservation is important so that history can be shared with future generations.

Shipwreck Pests

An invasive species is an organism that causes harm to the ecology or environment of an area where it's not native. Zebra mussels and quagga mussels are invasive species in the Great Lakes. They attach themselves to hard surfaces, such as rocks and the hulls of ships. Zebra and quagga mussels appeared in the Great Lakes several decades ago. They likely arrived with European ships.

Zebra and quagga mussels can create big problems for shipwreck preservation. They are sometimes layered several inches thick, making it difficult to identify a wreck and take measurements. Removing the mussels can damage the sunken vessels. Pieces of a wreck may also break off under the weight of mussel buildup. To stop the spread of these mussels, boaters should carefully clean their boats after taking them out of the water.

Zebra mussels are native to eastern Europe and western Russia. They likely first invaded the Great Lakes in the 1980s.

~ A Blessing or a Curse? ~

Zebra mussels aren't just harmful to shipwrecks; they're also harmful to other organisms that live in the waters they invade. However, there is one thing they do that shipwreck explorers may not mind. Zebra mussels are filter feeders, meaning they eat tiny particles that float in the water. This makes the water clearer, which makes it easier to spot shipwrecks. Still, zebra mussels take away food sources from native filter feeders, which can result in native species dying off. The harm zebra mussels bring generally outweighs the good.

Shipwrecks at Risk

Scientists think shipwreck decay may be linked to **climate change**. A warmer climate means less ice on the lakes, increased **evaporation**, and lower water levels.

This could leave shallow shipwrecks exposed to waves, ice, and air, which would make them decay faster. Climate change can also affect water quality, making it harder for divers to find and explore shipwrecks.

Many recreational and commercial vessels still sail the Great Lakes today. Thanks to improvements in safety and technology, there aren't nearly as many accidents as there once were.

Changing water levels may also cause lakebed sediment to shift, either revealing or burying wrecks. Newly exposed sites would be exciting discoveries, but problems arise if people can visit them too easily. Amateur divers can damage a site accidentally or take objects purposely.

We know a lot about some shipwrecks. However, experts think only about one-third of the ships lost on the Great Lakes in the last 400 years have been found. Many more are waiting to be discovered!

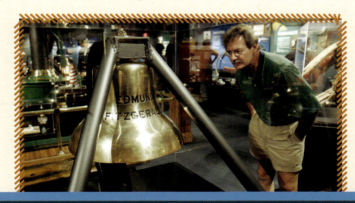

~ Maintaining History ~

With so many shipwrecks in the Great Lakes, it's not surprising that protected areas have been established to help preserve these important underwater archaeological sites. Thunder Bay in Lake Huron is just one of many protected areas. More than 200 shipwrecks have happened there. In some parts of the lakes, governments require special permits to dive to shipwrecks. Numerous Great Lakes museums also preserve and share the artifacts and stories of historical shipwrecks. Go to a museum and learn about more shipwreck history the next time you visit a Great Lake!

GLOSSARY

artifact: something made by humans in the past

climate change: change in Earth's long-term weather due in part to human activities such as burning oil and coal

disaster: something that happens suddenly and causes much suffering and loss for many people

document: to record something in writing, photography, or other form

environment: the natural world in which a plant or animal lives

evaporation: the process that changes a liquid, such as water, to a gas

habitat: the place or type of place where a plant or animal naturally or normally lives or grows

hurricane: a storm that begins over ocean waters and has strong winds and heavy rain

Industrial Revolution: a rapid major change in the economy in the 18th and 19th centuries marked by the introduction of power-driven machinery

remotely operated vehicle: an unoccupied underwater robot that is connected to a ship by cables

sonar: a way of using underwater sound waves to find objects or distances. Also, a type of machine that helps scientists explore the ocean by using sound waves.

technology: using science, engineering, and other industries to invent useful tools or to solve problems. Also a machine, piece of equipment, or method created by technology.

time capsule: a container that is filled with things from the present time and that is meant to be opened by people at some time in the future

For More Information

Books

Emminizer, Theresa. *Moving Ice: How the Great Lakes Formed.* New York, NY: PowerKids Press, 2020.

Silverman, Buffy. *Surviving a Shipwreck: The Titanic.* Minneapolis, MN: Lerner Publications, 2019.

Websites

Indiana Shipwrecks Virtual Tours
www.in.gov/dnr/lakemich/8526.htm
Take an online tour of four Lake Michigan shipwrecks.

Thunder Bay Wrecks
www.thunderbaywrecks.com/wrecks/
Go on a virtual diving journey of wrecks in the Thunder Bay area of Lake Huron, including the *Monohansett*.

What's So Great About the Great Lakes?
wonderopolis.org/wonder/whats-so-great-about-the-great-lakes
This page has even more information about the Great Lakes.

Publisher's note to educators and parents: Our editors have carefully reviewed these websites to ensure that they are suitable for students. Many websites change frequently, however, and we cannot guarantee that a site's future contents will continue to meet our high standards of quality and educational value. Be advised that students should be closely supervised whenever they access the internet.

INDEX

Argo 16, 17

Arthur M. Anderson 22

dredge 10

Edmund Fitzgerald 22, 23

Francisco Morazan 14

Herman H. Hettler 19

Hydrus 21

John V. Moran 4, 5

Lake Erie 6, 16, 17, 20, 24

Lake Huron 6, 18, 19, 20, 21, 24, 29

Lake Michigan 4, 5, 6, 7, 8, 11, 13, 14, 20, 24

Lake Ontario 6

Lake Superior 6, 9, 18, 19, 20, 22, 24

Lockwood, James 13

Monohansett 18, 19

Morania 17

Penobscot 17

quagga mussels 26

Rich, Craig 5

SS Eastland 7

SS Mataafa 9

SS Milwaukee 14, 15

Trotter, Dave 21

zebra mussels 26, 27